KAZ®
(Keyboarding A-Z)

Touch-Typing Quick and Easy

A Crisp Fifty-Minute™ Series Book

This Fifty-Minute™ Book is designed to be "read with a pencil." It is an excellent workbook for self-study as well as classroom learning. All material is copyright-protected and cannot be duplicated without permission from the publisher. *Therefore, be sure to order a copy for every training participant by contacting:*

1-800-442-7477 ◆ 25 Thomson Place, Boston, MA ◆ www.courseilt.com

KAZ® (Keyboarding A-Z)

Touch-Typing Quick and Easy

CREDITS:

Senior Editor:	**Debbie Woodbury**
Assistant Editor:	**Genevieve McDermott**
Production Manager:	**Denise Powers**
Design:	**Nicole Phillips**
Design Adaptation:	**Dan Quackenbush**
Gotham New Media Ltd:	**Mark Meakings**

KAZ® Typing Tutor produced by NETg under license from:

Gotham New Media Ltd
P.O. Box 23
Bexhill TN39 4ZU, UK
www.kaz.co.uk

For more information contact:

NETg
25 Thomson Place
Boston, MA 02210

Or find us on the Web at **www.courseilt.com**

For permission to use material from this text or product, submit a request online at: www.thomsonrights.com

Any additional questions about permissions can be submitted by e-mail to: thomsonrights@thomson.com

Trademarks

Crisp Fifty-Minute Series is a trademark of NETg.

KAZ is a trademark of Gotham New Media Ltd.

If mike jived, rude dunce, slap now, baggy hat, and *extra quiz* are trademarks of Gotham New Media Ltd.

Some of the product names and company names used in this book have been used for identification purposes only and may be trademarks or registered trademarks of their respective manufacturers and sellers.

Disclaimer

NETg reserves the right to revise this publication and make changes from time to time in its content without notice.

ISBN 1-4188-4108-0
Library of Congress Catalog Card Number 2004098348
Printed in the United States of America
2 3 4 5 08 07 06

Learning Objectives for

KAZ®
(KEYBOARDING A-Z)

The objectives for *KAZ® (Keyboarding A-Z)* are listed below. They have been developed to guide the user to the core issues covered in this book.

The objectives of this book are to help the user:

1) Use the keyboard with correct posture, and identify the home keys and their importance in touch-typing.
2) Touch-type all the letter keys.
3) Touch-type the letter keys with increased speed and accuracy.
4) Touch-type capital letters, special characters, and standard punctuation.
5) Touch-type numbers on a numeric keypad.
6) Develop speed and accuracy, and calculate typing speed in words per minute.

Assessing Progress

NETg has developed a Crisp Series **assessment** that covers the fundamental information presented in this book. A 25-item, multiple-choice and true/false questionnaire allows the reader to evaluate his or her comprehension of the subject matter.

To buy the assessment and answer key, go to www.courseilt.com and search on the book title or via the assessment format, or call 1-800-442-7477.

Assessments should not be used in any employee-selection process.

Introduction

The ability to touch-type using all 10 fingers is one of the most important skills required in today's computer-literate society. There's a significant difference in performance between people who touch-type with 10 fingers, looking at their screen, and people who look down at the keyboard and hunt for and peck the keys with two fingers. Touch-typists focus on the content of their work on screen without having to think about the keyboard. People who hunt and peck struggle to work at half speed, and their concentration is constantly broken. By using KAZ, you can significantly reduce the learning time needed to acquire the valuable skill of touch-typing.

The KAZ® Method

"KAZ" stands for "**K**eyboarding **A** to **Z**." The KAZ method of teaching typing was developed in the United Kingdom by Gotham New Media Ltd, with the goal of revolutionizing the way people learn how to type properly. Learning how to touch-type the core A-to-Z keys (alphabet keys) usually takes from 10 to 25 hours of boring, repetitive drills. With the KAZ method, you can learn how to touch-type the a-z keys in as little as 90 minutes, and you'll have a lot more fun in the process.

Before you start using the KAZ method, you'll need to understand the following:

- **How KAZ works** — The system introduces the different keys a few at a time and involves typing memorable phrases while you practice.
- **Proper keyboarding posture** — Good posture is critical to your ongoing success with the keyboard. Good posture can help prevent fatigue and soreness in your hands and wrists.

You'll learn about these concepts in the first section of the book. Before you get started, take the self-assessment on the following page to gain a better understanding of your current keyboarding skills.

EVALUATE YOUR SKILLS

To evaluate your familiarity with keyboarding skills, you can rate yourself on a scale of 1 to 5. The rating of 1 means this skill is new to you, 3 means it is somewhat familiar to you, and 5 means you are already skilled in this area.

Skill	1	2	3	4	5
Using correct posture while keyboarding					
Identifying the home keys					
Touch-typing the I, F, M, K, E, J, V, and D keys					
Touch-typing the Enter key and Spacebar					
Touch-typing the R, U, N, and C keys					
Touch-typing the S, L, A, P, O, and W keys					
Touch-typing the B, G, Y, H, and T keys					
Touch-typing the X, Q, and Z keys					
Touch-typing capital letters by using the Shift key					
Touch-typing special characters by using the Shift key					
Touch-typing the standard punctuation keys					
Touch-typing numbers on a numeric keypad					
Increasing touch-typing speed and accuracy					
Calculating typing speed in words per minute					

If you rated yourself 3 or lower on any of these items, you will greatly benefit from reading this book and practicing the KAZ method.

Table of Contents

P A R T **1**

Getting Started with KAZ

Benefits of the KAZ Method

The best things in life are simple, and the KAZ method was designed to be simple so that students can learn quickly. KAZ is a fresh, fast, and effective new approach to learning how to type. The critical aspects that have made KAZ a success are the way it introduces the keys and the memorable phrases that bind the skills together. KAZ offers you the following benefits that ensure efficient touch-typing:

- KAZ provides you with five key phrases designed to teach you how to touch-type all 26 letter keys in as little as 90 minutes.
- KAZ combines word association with natural dexterity to create a method that centers on five trademarked phrases. This method focuses on the way finger movements are learned across the keyboard and on the symmetry of keystrokes.
- Each section in the KAZ program offers encouragement and bite-sized instruction, enabling you to work at your own pace. You'll assimilate information and gain speed and accuracy without even realizing it.

Check (✓) the following keyboarding skills that you would like to achieve:

- ❑ Type without looking at the keyboard.
- ❑ Type accurate sentences.
- ❑ Increase typing speed.
- ❑ Prevent fatigue.
- ❑ Use 10 fingers to type.
- ❑ Quickly position your fingers on the keyboard.
- ❑ Use firm stroking of the keys.

Keyboarding Posture

When you're sitting at a keyboard, it's important to pay attention to your posture. Sitting in the proper position helps prevent fatigue and soreness in your hands and wrists.

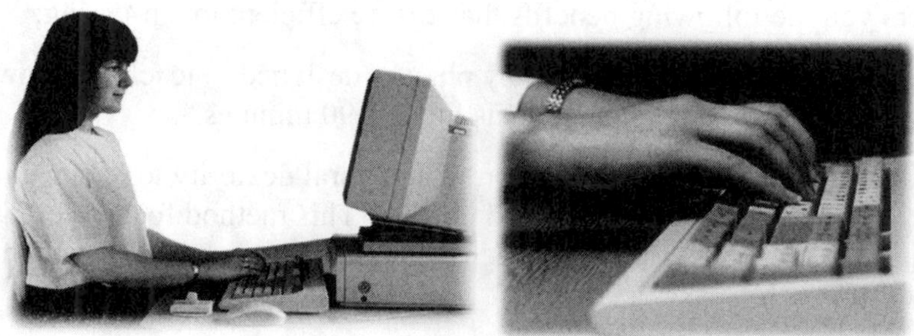

As you proceed through this course, follow these guidelines:

- When your hands rest on the keys, your fingers should be slightly curved. They should not stick out straight.
- Use a soft touch on the keys.
- Your elbows should rest lightly against your waist, and you should try to keep your wrists in line with your hands. This will make it easier to reach the keys.
- Adjust your chair so that your feet rest on the floor.
- Your arms should be approximately horizontal, and your eyes should be at the same height as the top of your monitor.
- Make sure there is enough space underneath your workstation to move your legs freely.
- Move any obstacles. Avoid excess pressure on the backs of your legs and knees. A footrest might also be helpful.
- Don't sit in the same position for long periods of time.

OBSERVING YOUR POSTURE

When sitting at your keyboard, should you:

	Yes	No
1. Stick your fingers out straight?	❑	❑
2. Use a hard touch on the keys?	❑	❑
3. Need to adjust your chair so that your feet rest on the floor?	❑	❑
4. Keep your arms horizontal (parallel to the floor)?	❑	❑
5. Keep your eyes at the same height as the top of your monitor?	❑	❑
6. Sit in the same position for long periods of time?	❑	❑

Compare your answers to the author's responses in the Appendix.

The Keyboard

This book is designed for use with a QWERTY keyboard. QWERTY simply refers to the first six letters in the main block of keys in the standard keyboard setup. If you look at your keyboard, you will see that the main block of keys is, for the most part, made up of the letters of the alphabet.

The other keys on the keyboard are numbers, punctuation characters, Shift, Caps Lock, and special characters.

The Home Row

The *home row* consist of the eight keys where you will place your fingers when you start to type. These keys form a base from which to move. The A, S, D, and F keys are pressed with the left hand. The J, K, L, and semicolon keys are pressed with the right hand.

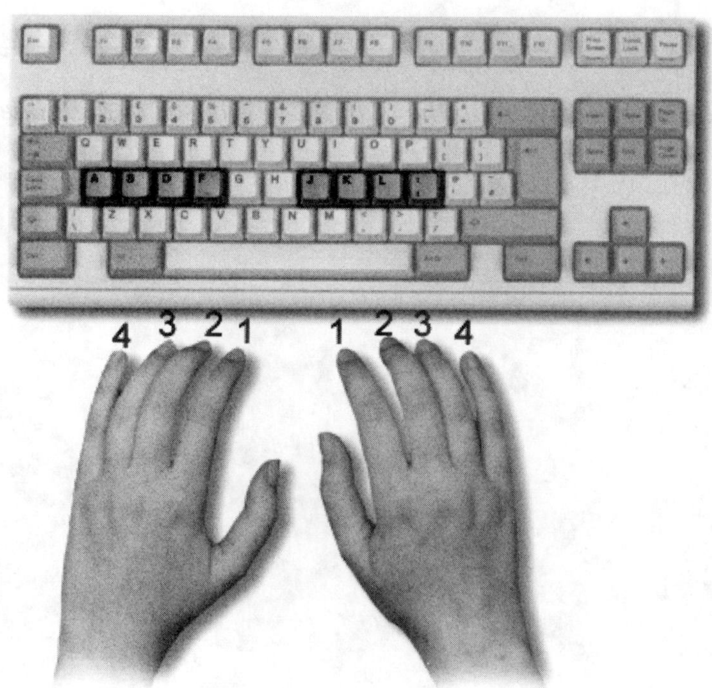

Look at the numbers in the preceding figure to see which finger to use for each key.

- **4** is your little finger, or "pinky" finger.
- **3** is your ring finger.
- **2** is your middle finger.
- **1** is your index finger.

You should rest these fingers on these keys when you are pausing between typing. As you reach for the other keys on the keyboard, your fingers will return to these home keys naturally.

Tip: ***The F and J keys have raised dots or ridges that provide tactile feedback that your fingers are on the correct keys.***

The ridges on the F and J keys preclude the need to look down at the keyboard to verify that your fingers are on the correct keys. You will find that to operate a keyboard efficiently, you must identify the correct placement of your hands and fingers by touch.

IDENTIFYING THE HOME ROW

1. With your eyes closed, place your left index finger on the F key.
2. With your eyes closed, place your right index finger on the J key.
3. With your eyes still closed, verify that you can feel the raised ridges on these keys.
4. With your eyes still closed, let your other fingers rest on the remaining home keys.
5. With your eyes still closed, press each home key one at a time, from left to right.
6. Open your eyes and verify that you have typed **a**, **s**, **d**, **f**, **j**, **k**, **l**, and **;**.

PART 2

The Five Key Phrases

Using the Key Phrases

The KAZ program uses five key phrases. These phrases are specially designed to cover all 26 letter keys with virtually symmetrical movements, so that one hand mirrors the other hand. These phrases provide progressively challenging exercises that, when practiced repeatedly, will help you automatically locate each key on the keyboard.

For maximum effectiveness, it's recommended that you practice touch-typing all of the key phrases in the following order:

1. **if mike jived** — The first phrase will introduce you to typing some letter keys as well as other keys.

2. **rude dunce** — This phrase introduces four new alpha (letter) keys. You'll also practice the letters you have already learned.

3. **slap now** — This phrase follows a flow while you're typing so that you remember which fingers are to be used.

4. **baggy hat** — Typing this phrase, you'll use mainly your index fingers.

5. **extra quiz** — Typing this phrase takes more time than typing other phrases because it introduces the three letters that are least used.

As you can see, all five phrases consist of multiple words. While practicing these phrases, you'll need to observe the cursor and use some keys other than the alpha keys. These keys are Spacebar and Enter.

The Cursor

The *cursor* is a standard on-screen symbol in word processing programs. It is the vertical blinking line that indicates your location in the document. Typing a letter or a space will move the cursor to the right, following the characters you type. The blinking helps you quickly identify where you are in the document.

The Spacebar

The *Spacebar* is located below the other keys. It's the long key with no label. Depending on your keyboard and operating system, your Spacebar might look slightly different from the one shown below.

You use the Spacebar to create spaces between words or letters. Use your right thumb to press the Spacebar. You should be able to reach it without taking your fingers off the home keys.

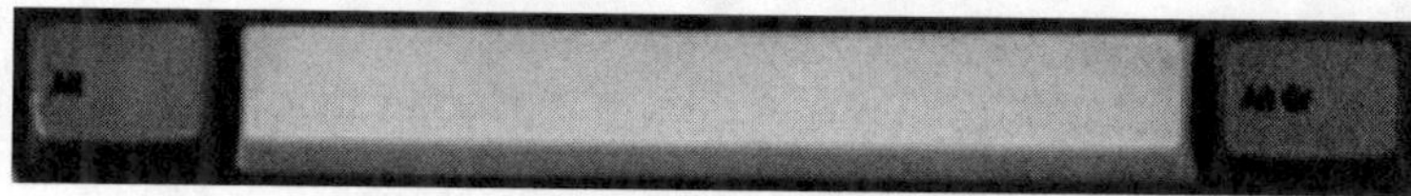

Typing the First Key Phrase

The first key phrase is *if mike jived.* This phrase contains three words, which means that you'll need to use the Spacebar in addition to the eight unique letters in the phrase. The keys in this phrase are shown in the following figure:

Watch the screen as you type. The letters that appear will provide confirmation that you are pressing the correct keys.

The first thing you should do is to keep your fingers on the home row so that it's convenient for you to reach all eight keys. To type this phrase, you'll use your first and second fingers of both hands.

TYPING *if mike*

Here's how:	Here's why:
1. Without looking down at the keyboard, place the fingers of both hands on the home keys	
With the second finger of your right hand, reach up from `K` and press `I`, without looking down at the keyboard	

2. With the first finger of your left hand, press F

You have now completed the first word: "if."

3. With your fingers resting lightly on the home keys, reach down with your right thumb to press the Spacebar once

To create a space between the word "if" and the next word in the phrase.

Observe that the cursor moves one space to the right

4. Taking your time, type **if** and then a space, and do this several times

Type this over and over again until you feel the action become automatic. Don't worry about making a mistake. That's expected at this early stage.

After you have typed these characters several times, observe that the characters automatically flow down to the next line on the screen

This feature is known as "word wrap." The lines in your document are created automatically, so you don't have to worry about reaching the right edge of the document when you type.

5. With your hands resting on the home keys, slowly reach down with your right index finger and press M

To type the first letter in the word "mike."

6. Taking your time, type **if m** several times	(Be sure to include a space between "if" and "m" and between each instance of "if m.") Type this until you feel the action become automatic.
7. Type **if mi** several times	Put a space between "if" and "mi" each time.
With the second finger of your right hand, press K a few times, inserting a space between each letter	K is one of the home keys. Remember to look at the screen, not down at the keyboard, as you type.
8. Type **if mik** several times	Keep typing until the sequence feels automatic.
9. With your fingers resting on the home keys, use the second finger of your left hand to reach up and press E	
10. Press E several times, with a space between each letter	To practice locating the E key and the Spacebar.
11. With your fingers resting on the home keys, type **mike** several times, with a space between each word	Don't rush yourself. It's better to start with a slow, rhythmic pace than a hurried, inaccurate pace.
12. Type **if mike** several times, with a space between each word	Repeat these two words until typing them feels automatic.

The Enter Key

The *Enter* key moves the cursor down one line and repositions it along the left margin of the document. Press the Enter key to create new lines or paragraphs. Use your right pinky finger to press the Enter key.

TYPING *if mike jived*

Here's how:	Here's why:
1. Rest your fingers on the home keys	
With your right index finger, press `J`	The J key is one of the home keys. It has a raised ridge on it to help orient you to the home row.
2. With the second finger of your right hand, reach up and press `I`	You're already familiar with the I key.
3. Using the first and second fingers of your right hand, type **ji** several times	You can add a space between each pair of letters if you choose. Type these two letters until the sequence feels automatic.
4. With the index finger of your left hand, reach down and press `V`	You can also practice moving your finger down without pressing the V key.
With your fingers resting on the home keys, type **jiv** several times, with a space between each instance	Make sure you use your right index finger for the J, your second finger (of the right hand) for the I, and your left index finger for the V key.
5. With the second finger of your left hand, reach up and press `E`	
Bring the same finger back to its home row position and press `D`	

6. Type **ed** several times	Make sure you press both keys with the same finger, as shown in the previous picture.
7. Type **jived** several times, with a space between each word	Repeat the word until you feel the action become automatic.
8. With your fingers resting on the home keys, type **if mike jived** four times	Remember to look at your screen, not down at your hands, and to insert a space between each word.
9. With your right pinky finger (your fourth finger), press ⏎, and then return your right hand to the home keys	Feel free to look down at the keyboard as you press the Enter key for the first few times. When you think the action is automatic, repeat this step without looking at the keyboard.
Press ⏎ again and return your fingers to the home keys	
Repeat this four more times	

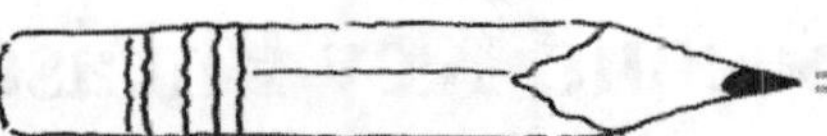

CHECK YOUR UNDERSTANDING

After you have practiced typing the first phrase, *if mike jived*, answer the following questions:

1. How do you insert a space between words?

   ____

2. Which finger do you use to press the Spacebar?

   ____

3. How does a cursor help while you're typing?

   ____

4. How do you move the cursor to the next line?

   ____

5. Which finger do you use to press the Enter key?

   ____

Compare your answers to the author's responses in the Appendix.

Typing the Second Key Phrase

Typing the phrase *rude dunce* will help you automatically locate the R, U, N, and C keys.

You might think this is a strange phrase to practice, but remember that these word combinations are specially designed to teach you the keyboard in sequence. The phrase *rude dunce* contains two letters that you're already familiar with typing: D and E. As you learn to locate the other letters in this phrase without looking at the keyboard, you will also practice keys you already know.

***Tip:* Remember to press the Spacebar with your right thumb.**

TYPING *rude*

Here's how:	Here's why:
1. With your fingers resting on the home keys, reach up with your left index finger and press R, as shown	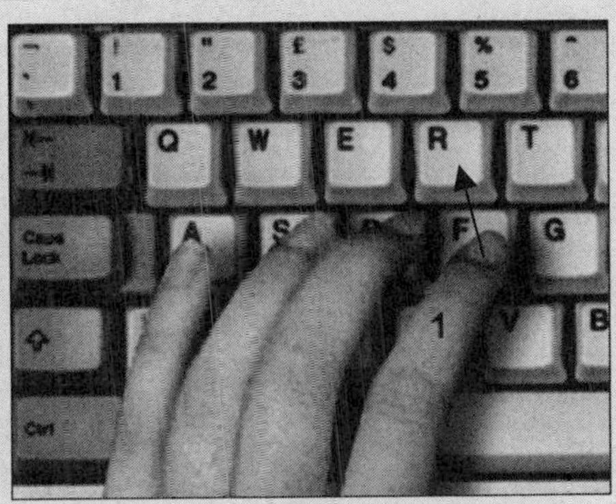
Press this key several times, inserting a space between each letter	Remember to use your right thumb to press the Spacebar.
2. With your right index finger, reach up from the J home key and press U, as shown	
Press U several times, and insert a space between each letter 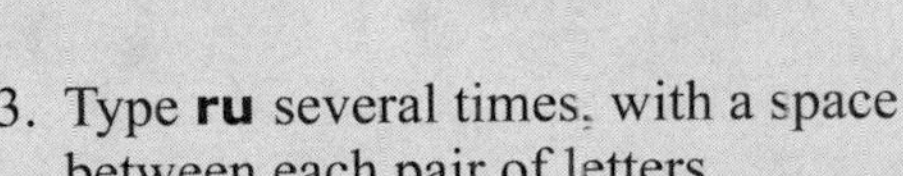	
3. Type **ru** several times, with a space between each pair of letters	
4. With the second finger of your left hand, press D	D is a home key you should feel comfortable with at this point.
Reach up from D and press E with the same finger	
Type **de** several times, with a space between each pair	
5. Type **rude** several times, with a space between each word	Remember, don't look down at the keys.

Completing the Phrase

Now, you'll type the word "dunce" to complete the second phrase in the KAZ program. This word contains only two new letters: N and C. To press the N key, you use your right index finger. To press the C key, you use the second finger of your right hand.

TYPING *rude dunce*

Here's how:	Here's why:
1. With your fingers resting on the home keys, press D	Use the second finger of your left hand.
With your right index finger, reach up and press U	You should feel comfortable locating this key without looking at the keyboard.
2. Type **du** several times, with a space between each pair of letters	
3. With your right index finger, reach down and press N	
4. Type **dun** several times, with a space between each instance	

5. With the second finger of your left hand, reach down and press c several times, slowly

6. Press e

To start a new line.

7. Type the word **dunce** several times, with a space between each word

You're already familiar with typing the E key in three different words. It's okay if you make a few mistakes.

8. Type **rude dunce** several times, with a space between each word

Concentrate on accuracy rather than speed.

9. Type **if rude mike jived** several times, with a space between each word

Type slowly while looking at your screen.

10. Check your posture

    Verify that you are not slouching, and that your elbows are resting lightly against your waist

    Your fingers should be curved slightly and resting on the home keys

11. Type **if mike jived** four times, and press e after each phrase

12. Type **rude dunce** four times, and press e after each phrase

Typing the Third Key Phrase

So far, you have learned to touch-type almost half of the alpha keys. The third key phrase in the KAZ program is *slap now.*

Yes, this is another silly phrase, but remember, it was specially designed to involve sequential, symmetrical finger movements. The phrase *slap now* involves new keys and new fingers, but you will likely find that they are no more difficult than the keys you have already used. You will use the third and fourth fingers of both hands to complete this phrase.

TYPING *slap now*

Here's how:	Here's why:
1. Close your eyes and place your fingers on the home keys	
2. With the third finger of your left hand, press S	Remember to keep your eyes closed.
Open your eyes and look at your screen	Verify that you have typed the letter "s." If you didn't press the right key, don't worry about it. It will soon become automatic.
3. Press S several times, with a space between each letter	Use your left ring finger (your third finger). 
4. With your right ring finger (your third finger), press L	
5. Type **sl** several times, with a space between each pair of letters	Use the third finger on each hand.

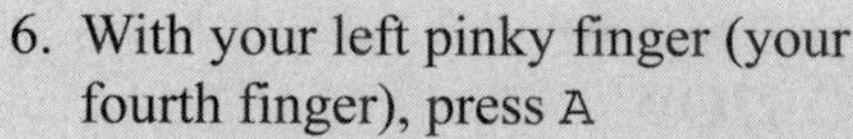

6. With your left pinky finger (your fourth finger), press A

7. Type **sla** four times, with a space between each instance

8. With your right pinky (your fourth finger), reach up and press P

   Bring your right pinky back to its home key, and then press P

   Repeat this step four times

9. Type **slap** four times, with a space between each word

   Make sure you look at the screen, not down at the keyboard.

   Press e, and then type **slap** another four times, with a space between each word

   The fingering is left ring finger, right ring finger, left pinky, right pinky up.

10. Which finger do you use to type N?

    You use your right index finger.

11. With your fingers resting on the home keys, reach down and press `N` a few times

    Press `N` again, followed by a space

    Use your right thumb to press the Spacebar.

12. With your right ring finger (your third finger), reach up from the home key and press `O`

13. With your left ring finger, reach up from the home key and press `W`

14. Type **ow** four times, with a space between each pair of letters

    Type **now** four times, with a space between each word

15. Type **slap now** four times, with a space between each phrase

    Repeat this phrase until the typing action is automatic

Typing the Fourth Key Phrase

Hopefully, you're starting to feel more comfortable locating the keys you've learned so far. Of the 26 letters in the alphabet, there are only eight keys you haven't learned yet. Now, you'll learn the next key phrase to practice: *baggy hat*.

To type this phrase, you will need to learn five new keys: B, G, Y, H, and T. You'll use your index fingers to type all the letters in this phrase except for A.

The first word, *baggy*, starts with the B key, which involves a larger reach than you have made so far. To press the B key, you stretch your left index finger down and slightly inside.

Error! Objects cannot be created from editing field codes.

You'll also need to reach to press the Y key. To press the Y key, stretch your right index finger up and slightly inside.

Error! Objects cannot be created from editing field codes.

TYPING *baggy hat*

Here's how:	Here's why:
1. Move your left index finger from its home position down to B	
Practice making this move from F to B a few times	It's okay if you look at the keyboard while you practice this move.
2. Type **ab** four times, with a space between each pair of letters	
3. Type **fb** four times, with a space between each pair of letters	
4. Type **ab fb** four times	Take it slowly and focus on your accuracy. Remember to look at the screen and return your fingers to their home keys after you press each key.

5. With your fingers on the home keys, move your left index finger across to press G, as shown

6. Type **bag** several times, with a space between each word
7. With your fingers on the home keys, reach up with your right index finger and press Y

It's okay if you look at the keyboard to press Y for the first time.

Type **ggy** four times, with a space between each instance

8. Type **baggy** several times, with a space between each word

Type "b" with your left index finger, "a" with your left pinky finger, "g" with your left index finger, and "y" with your right index finger.

9. With your right index finger, reach across to press H, as shown

Type **ha** four times, with a space between each pair of letters

Use your left pinky finger to press the A key.

10. With your left index finger, reach up from its home key and press T, as shown

Repeat the action of moving from the home key position to T several times

11. Type **hat** four times, with a space between each word

12. Type **baggy hat** several times, with a space between each phrase

Type this phrase until the action is automatic. Take your time and concentrate on accuracy.

Typing the Fifth Key Phrase

You've come a long way, and there are only three new keys to learn. The final key phrase in the KAZ program is *extra quiz.* The new letters in this phrase are X, Q, and Z.

In this phrase, you might find that the X, Q, and Z keys are the hardest to locate by touch-typing. Take some extra time with these keys. They are a little more difficult to touch-type than the others, but they are also the least frequently used letters in the alphabet. Eventually, you will find these keys as automatically as you find your home keys.

Tip: ***Type this phrase slowly, and reinforce the required finger movements.***

To press the Q key, you will reach up with your left pinky finger.

To press the Z key, you will use the same finger, but you will reach down and slightly inside. To press the X key, you'll reach down and slightly inside with your left ring finger (your third finger).

These moves will likely feel the most awkward of all the keys you have learned so far. Don't worry; they will soon be second nature to you, as with the other keys. It's a bit like learning how to drive; you start by learning the controls, and through repeated practice, using the controls becomes second nature. You work the controls without having to think about your actions. Eventually, with a lot of practice, touch-typing all the keys in the alphabet will feel automatic.

TYPING *extra quiz*

Here's how:	Here's why:
1. With your fingers resting on the home keys, press E with the second finger of your left hand, as shown	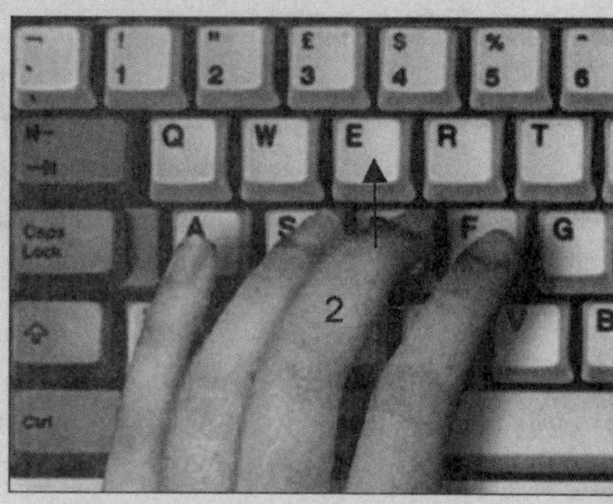
2. With your left ring finger (your third finger), reach down and slightly inside to press X Practice pressing X several times, returning your left ring finger to its home key each time	Look at your screen and verify that you have pressed the right key.
3. Type **ex** four times, with a space between each pair of letters	
4. Type **tra** four times, with a space between each instance	You're already familiar with these keys.
5. Type **extra** several times, with a space between each word	Repeat this word, slowly, until typing it begins to feel comfortable. Don't worry about making mistakes. Just try to feel the correct sequence and location of each key.

6. With your fingers resting on the home keys, reach up with your left pinky finger and press Q

7. Type **ui** four times, with a space between each pair of letters

   You're already familiar with the U and I keys.

8. Type **qui** four times, with a space between each instance

   Go slowly, and look at your screen to verify that you are pressing the correct keys.

9. With your left pinky finger, reach down and slightly inside to press Z

   Type **uiz** four times, with a space between each instance

10. Type **quiz** several times, with a space between each word

    Repeat this word, slowly, until typing it begins to feel comfortable.

11. Type **extra quiz** several times, with a space between each phrase

    Don't worry about making mistakes. Just try to feel the correct sequence and location of each key. Repeat the phrase until you can type it accurately several times in a row.

TYPING KEY PHRASES

1. With your fingers resting on the home keys and your eyes focused on your screen, type the following phrases four times each. Insert a space between each word, and start each phrase on a new line by pressing the Enter key.
   - **if mike jived**
   - **rude dance**
   - **slap now**
   - **baggy hat**
   - **extra quiz**
2. Type **slap mike now** several times, until it feels automatic and you have no errors three times in a row.
3. Type **if baggy hat dance** several times, until it feels automatic and you have no errors three times in a row.
4. Type **rude dance hat** several times, until it feels automatic and you have no errors three times in a row.
5. Type **baggy dunce hat** several times, until it feels automatic and you have no errors three times in a row.
6. Try mixing up the keywords to make your own phrases, even if they're complete nonsense.

PART 3

Words and Sentences

Typing with the First Two Fingers

You've successfully made it through all the alphabet keys. Now you're ready to begin practicing other words that will help you touch-type more accurately. In this topic, you will practice typing words that involve using the first two fingers on each hand.

Words That Involve Using Your First Two Fingers

To get started, you will type some simple words combining some of the letters of the first two key phrases you have learned, *if mike jived* and *rude dunce*. Practicing in this way will help your touch-typing skills become progressively more automatic.

There are so many words you can type using the first two fingers. To begin with, you can practice typing the following words three times each, with a space between each word:

creed	fence	mend
crime	fend	mere
deem	feud	mice
deer	fever	mike
dice	find	mind
diced	five	murder
did	freed	need
died	fried	never
dive	if	nice
drink	jived	rice
dunce	kid	rude
feed	kin	rum

Tip: ***Concentrate on developing your typing rhythm and accuracy. Don't worry about speed at this stage. This will come with practice.***

Observe Mistakes

Type more words such as *fried, rum,* and *drink* to practice typing with the first two fingers. Are you making any consistent mistakes? When you make consistent mistakes in typing letters, it's a good idea to practice typing those letters (and words using those letters) repeatedly.

Typing with the First, Third, and Fourth Fingers

You have now practiced touch-typing several words that involve the first two fingers on each hand. In this topic, you will continue to develop your touch-typing skills by practicing words that involve the first, third, and fourth fingers on each hand.

Words That Involve Your First, Third, and Fourth Fingers

Remember the phrases *slap now* and *baggy hat*? Typing these phrases required using your first, third, and fourth fingers. You will now practice touch-typing other words that involve these fingers.

Type the following words three times each, with a space after each word:

bag	**hang**	**salt**
baggy	**happy**	**sang**
ball	**hat**	**slap**
bang	**hog**	**slay**
bats	**host**	**slow**
blast	**hot**	**soggy**
gang	**last**	**song**
gasp	**long**	**stab**
ghost	**pall**	**stag**
glow	**pang**	**stall**
gnat	**plan**	**tag**
hag	**play**	**tall**
hall	**post**	**toast**
halt	**sag**	**what**

After practicing typing the list of words on the previous page, answer the following questions:

1. Did you look at the screen while typing?
2. Did you feel your speed improving?
3. Did you find it easy to locate the keys without looking at the keyboard?
4. Did you get confused about which finger should be used for a particular key?

Typing with the Third and Fourth Fingers of the Left Hand

In this topic, you will continue to develop your touch-typing skills by practicing words that contain the letters you used in the key phrase *extra quiz*.

Words That Involve the Third and Fourth Fingers of the Left Hand

You might find typing with the third and fourth fingers of your left hand a little trickier because those fingers aren't used as often, and therefore they're not as strong as your other fingers. Keep in mind that typing "awkward" keys will eventually become as easy to you as using the keys in the home row.

Type the following words three times each, with a space between each word:

exact	**quiet**
excite	**quit**
exit	**quite**
extra	**quiz**
haze	**raze**
laze	**relax**
lazy	**taxi**
maze	**teal**
quad	**zoo**
quart	**tazer**
quick	

Typing Sentences

Had enough of random words and nonsense phrases? Now you'll practice your touch-typing skills by typing complete sentences. Don't worry about punctuation and capitalization yet—you'll learn those keys later in this course.

Type the following sentences three times each, with one line between each sentence:

- **come to the shops with me**
- **please clean your room**
- **dance this way**
- **drive this car today**
- **jane walked to and from school**
- **he pretends to cry**
- **be extra quiet in class**
- **she wants to go to the zoo**
- **the dog jumped back up**
- **mike opened his present**
- **play golf today**
- **hang out the washing please**
- **catch the taxi**
- **the sun was hot**
- **walk very quickly down the stairs**
- **jane was lazy**

Tip: ***Don't forget to use the Enter key when typing sentences on different lines.***

Measuring Your Progress

Congratulations, you've come a long way! You can always measure your progress by going back and typing the key phrases you learned earlier. You'll probably notice that you can type these phrases faster and with greater accuracy. As you continue to practice your touch-typing, revisit these phrases from time to time to gauge your progress.

Measuring Progress

- ***if mike jived***
- ***rude dunce***
- ***slap now***
- ***baggy hat***
- ***extra quiz***

Did you type these phrases faster and more accurately than the last time you typed them?

Tip: ***There is only one way to become an effective touch-typist: practice, practice, practice.***

TYPING WORDS AND SENTENCES

1. Type the following words two or three times each, or until they feel automatic:

   crime deem dice drink feed find fever fried mend rice rum

2. Type the following words two or three times each, or until they feel automatic:

   ball blast gang glow ghost happy host sloppy salt

3. Type the following words two or three times each, or until they feel automatic:

   extra haze quick quart quiet quiz taxi tazer

4. Type the following sentences two or three times each, or until they feel automatic:

   - **catch the taxi**
   - **play golf today**
   - **jane was lazy**
   - **mike opened his present**

PART 4

Capitalization, Numbers, and Punctuation

Using Capital Letters

The next step in the development of your touch-typing skills is to use the Shift key. When you press and hold the Shift key, all letters you type become capitals, which are essential in any written language. In this topic, you'll learn how to touch-type capital letters by using the Shift key.

The Shift Key

Most standard keyboards have two Shift keys so you can use either hand, depending on preference or on the location of the key you're shifting. The Shift keys are always located on both ends of the bottom row of letter keys. The shaded keys in the figure below are examples of the two Shift keys. Most Shift keys have an up-pointing arrow, and one or both Shift keys are elongated. You use your pinky fingers (the fourth finger on each hand) to press the Shift keys.

Typing Capital Letters

To type capital letters, you need to press and hold the Shift key and then press the desired letter key. This might seem difficult at first, but with practice you'll find it simple, and you won't need to think about it as you go.

If you need to type a key that's on the right side of the keyboard, use your left pinky finger to hold down the left Shift key. If you need to type a key that's on the left side of the keyboard, use your right pinky finger to hold down the right Shift key.

Tip: ***When you press the Shift key, make sure you don't take your fingers off the home keys.***

Many touch-typists develop their own preference for how they use the Shift key, and you might do the same over a period of time. Some typists prefer always to use one Shift key, no matter which letter they need to capitalize.

USING THE SHIFT KEY

Here's how:	Here's why:
1. With your fingers resting lightly on the home keys, reach down and slightly outward with your left pinky finger to press `s`	
Practice the motion of moving your pinky from `A` to `s` a few times	
2. Use your left pinky finger to press and hold `s`	
Press `I`	
3. Do you see a capital I on your screen? If not, try again	
4. On the next line, type **If Mike jived**	Press the Enter key to move to the next line.
Type **If Mike jived** a few more times	

5. With your fingers resting on the home keys, reach across with your right pinky finger to press the other s key

Practice the motion of moving your pinky finger from the semicolon key to s a few times

6. Use your right pinky finger to press and hold s

Press R

On the next line, type
Rude dunce

Type **Rude dunce** a few more times

Practice typing this phrase until the motion feels more comfortable.

Typing Capital Letters

Now that you're a little more familiar with the Shift key, you'll practice typing complete sentences with proper capitals, as well as a few abbreviations that consist of multiple capital letters.

Here's how:	Here's why:
1. With your fingers resting on the home keys, type **Slap Now**	Use the right Shift key for the letter S and the left Shift key for the letter N.
On the next line, type **Slap Now** a few more times	Go slowly. Your goals are still to improve accuracy and to get familiar with the keyboard.
2. On the next line, type **Baggy Hat** a few times	Use the right Shift key for the letter B and the left Shift key for the letter H.
3. On the next line, type **Extra Quiz** a few times	Use the right Shift key for both capital letters.
4. Type the following phrases three times each: **If Mike Jived** **Rude Dunce** **Slap Now** **Baggy Hat** **Extra Quiz**	Don't worry about making errors. Your goal is to develop a feel for the Shift key that is as automatic as the home keys.

Caps Lock

The *Caps Lock* key locks the letters so that they appear as capital letters until you press the Caps Lock key again. The Caps Lock key is a *toggle switch*, which means that pressing it once activates it and pressing it again deactivates it. On most keyboards, a small light will turn on, indicating that Caps Lock is activated. Caps Lock is useful when you want all your text to be uppercase, such as for headlines and other noticeable text in documents like flyers and newsletters.

Use your left pinky finger to press the Caps Lock key. It's a similar motion to pressing the left Shift key, but you move your pinky finger directly across to the left, instead of across and slightly downward.

USING CAPS LOCK

To practice typing capital letters by using the Caps Lock key, type the following phrases:

- **IF MIKE JIVED**
- **RUDE DUNCE**
- **SLAP NOW**
- **BAGGY HAT**
- **EXTRA QUIZ**

Typing Capital Letters Intermittently

When you need to type consecutive capital letters and then return to lowercase letters, you have two options. If you prefer to use the Caps Lock key, you can turn it on and off as needed. Or, you can hold down the Shift key and type the letters you need, and then take your pinky finger off the Shift key to return to lowercase letters. Eventually, you will decide which option feels more comfortable to you.

Tip: ***It's usually preferable to use Caps Lock when you're typing an entire phrase in capital letters. Use the Shift key when you're capitalizing only the first letter in a word or sentence.***

Try to determine your own preference for using Caps Lock or pressing the Shift key to type consecutive capital letters.

Typing Sentences with Capital Letters

1. With your fingers resting on the home keys, type the following sentences three times each:
   - **The dog JUMPED up**
   - **Play GOLF Today**
   - **The SUN was HOT**
   - **Walk Quickly Down The Stairs**
   - **MIKE WAS HERE**
   - **Catch The TAXI**
   - **Jane works for NASA**
2. Do you prefer using the Caps Lock key or holding down the Shift key? Describe why you think one way is easier than the other.

Using the Number Row

Often, you'll need to type numbers along with your text. On most standard keyboards, you have the option of using the number row along the top of the keyboard or using the numeric keypad on the right side of the alphabet keys. In this topic, you will learn about the number row.

Typing Numbers

The number keys are a longer stretch from the home row, but with time, you'll be able to type the numbers you need with accuracy and speed. Even many experienced typists are not as accurate with the number keys as they are with the alphabet keys, so feel free to glance down at your keyboard as you type numbers. It's not as important or realistic to touch-type the number keys or to assign specific fingers to each key, because the number keys are not used extensively and the reach involved can be difficult for many people.

Try to concentrate on keeping your fingers on the home keys while you type numbers. If you take your fingers off the home keys, you will lose your orientation to the keyboard, and this can cost you speed and accuracy while you type words and numbers intermittently.

Some keyboards also have a numeric keypad: a second set of number keys to the far right of the alphabet keys. Some typists find it easier to use the numeric keypad because of its compact arrangement, but you're likely to develop your own preference for typing numbers.

Typing Numbers with Letters

1. With your fingers resting on the home keys, type the following sentences and phrases:

   - **11 men played cricket**
   - **Only 2 can go**
   - **7 divided by 3**
   - **4 boys and 3 girls went to school**
   - **94 books were overdue**
   - **39 people came to the meeting**
   - **He climbed 61 steps that day**

2. Repeat these sentences and phrases a few more times, or until the action feels automatic.

Shift Key Characters

Take a look at the characters above the number keys. These are called *Shift key characters*. To type them, you need to press and hold the Shift key. It's not important to learn how to touch-type these characters, because you won't use them nearly as often as the alphabet keys, and they involve a stretch that is difficult for most people.

Note: Some keys are in different locations, depending on the make of the keyboard and the country in which it's sold. Still, you should have a general understanding of the keys' locations so you can type these characters without too much hesitation.

TYPING SHIFT KEY CHARACTERS

1. Type the various Shift key characters several times, at your own pace. With the exception of the Shift key, don't worry about which fingers you use.
2. Practice typing a few of your own sentences that involve the Shift key characters.

Using Punctuation Keys

Punctuation is a critical part of touch-typing. To be a fast, accurate typist, you'll need to punctuate your sentences as automatically as you type letters. In this topic, you'll learn how to touch-type the most frequently used punctuation keys: comma, period, and semicolon.

Comma, Period, and Semicolon

Some punctuation keys involve the use of the Shift key, and some involve just the key itself. The semicolon key is perhaps the easiest punctuation key because it's one of the home keys. The comma and period do not require the Shift key either, and they are no more difficult to reach than some of the other letters you've already learned.

These three common punctuation keys involve the right hand. For the semicolon key, use your right pinky finger. The semicolon is a home key, so your finger should already be resting on it. All you need to do is press it. To touch-type the comma key, use the second finger of your right hand. For the period key, use your third finger.

Punctuation Keys Involving the Shift Key

You've probably noticed that some keys have two symbols on them. The bottom symbol is the default key. The top symbol is the Shift alternate for that key. For example, if you need to type a question mark, you need to press Shift+**?**, because the question mark is the alternate on the forward-slash key.

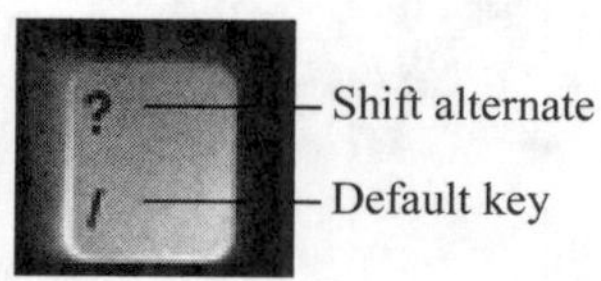

The colon is the Shift alternate of the semicolon, which is a home key. The double quotation mark is the Shift alternate of the apostrophe (the single-quote key), and the exclamation point is the Shift alternate of the number-1 key.

USING PUNCTUATION WHILE TYPING PHRASES

1. Type the following sentences and phrases. Follow the exact capitalization and punctuation provided for each one. Don't worry if they take some time. The keys are still new to you, and you will need to practice your new skill several times before it becomes automatic.

   - **The lady's handbag was brown.**
   - **Mike's hat was lost.**
   - **He lives in WINCHESTER.**
   - **Jane was quite upset, and decided to:**
   - **18 BOYS: 13 GIRLS**
   - **The Man in the Moon**
   - **The villa was $550 for ONE week's rental.**
   - **"Peter asked you to call him in the morning."**
   - **Jones, Bloggs & Smith, 98 Church Road, EXETER.**
   - **The room has an area of 15 square miles.**
   - **"Don't forget to add a 10% surcharge," said Mary's brother.**

2. Now see how automatic your typing is with the original five key phrases.

P A R T **5**

The Numeric Keypad

Playing with Numbers

You're already familiar with the number row above the letter keys. Many keyboards also have a numeric keypad, which is designed to improve your ability to touch-type numbers. In this topic, you will learn how to touch-type number keys on a numeric keypad.

Numeric Keypads

Some numeric keypads are extensions of keyboards, while other keypads are built in. When you're entering numbers, especially accounting figures, accuracy is critical. Numeric keypads improve your ability to type numbers fast and accurately, because the numeric keys above the letter keys are a big reach and it's easy to make mistakes with them.

A typical numeric keypad looks like the one shown below:

You'll need only your right hand to cover all the keys on a numeric keypad. The finger assignments are divided into four columns. The home keys on a numeric keypad aren't as standard as the alphabetical home keys. On some keypads, the 5 key has a raised ridge, like the F and J keys. This would indicate that the 4, 5, and 6 keys are the home keys. However, many people consider the 1, 2, and 3 keys to be the home keys for a keypad, so it's best that you develop your own preference for where your fingers rest on the keypad as you type.

The finger assignment for the numeric keypad is shown in the figure below:

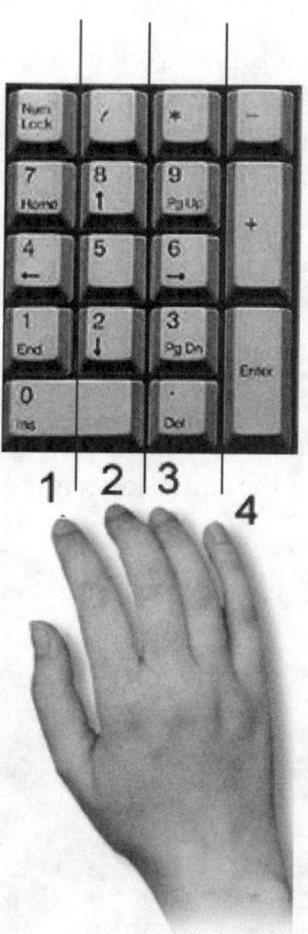

Tip: ***The 5 key has a raised ridge and thus can be used as a home key.***

Use your first finger to press the 1, 4, and 7 keys. Use your second finger to type the 0, 2, 5, 8, and forward slash keys. Use your third finger to type the decimal point, 3, 6, 9, and asterisk (*) keys. Finally, use your fourth finger to press the Enter, plus, and minus keys. When you're working with a numeric keypad, it's important to look at your screen as you type, so you can verify your accuracy.

TYPING NUMBERS

With your first three fingers resting on your numeric home keys, type the following lines of numbers:

- **1122112211**
- **1133113322**
- **2233113322**
- **4455665544**
- **7788998877**

Num Lock

Most keypads have a Num Lock key, which is a toggle switch that enables and disables the keypad. When the keypad is enabled, the Num Lock indicator light should appear.

Exploring the Numeric Keypad

1. Do you think you have a preference between using the number keys and using the numeric keypad? If so, describe why you think one way is easier than the other.

   ____

   ____

2. Press the Num Lock key and verify that the light is on. If a light turns on, press it again.

The Tab and Enter Keys

The numeric keypad has its own Enter key, which makes it easy to start a new line as you're typing numbers. The Tab key is also commonly used to add space between text or a series of numbers. The Tab key is located to the left of the Q key. You can use your left pinky finger (fourth finger) to press the Tab key as you type numbers on the numeric keypad.

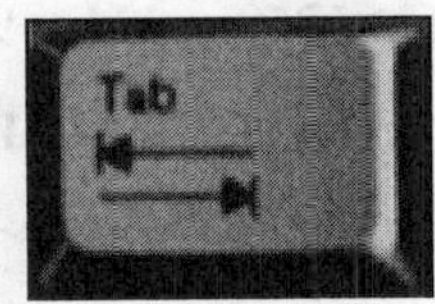

TYPING NUMBERS WITH SPACES

With your first three fingers resting on your numeric home keys, type the following numbers. To create spaces, press t wherever <> is written.

- **124<>1556<>8494<>546<>1258<>234<>987**
- **1.23<>3.94<>8.31<>87.67<>65.92<>34.71<>6.78**
- **351<>783<>345<>348<>927<>403<>910<>683**
- **4569<>9273<>6732<>5684<>9647<>3245**

P A R T 6

Speed and Accuracy

Improving Speed and Accuracy

Now that you have acquired the fundamental skills for touch-typing, you can work to develop your speed and accuracy. In this topic, you will warm up with short phrases, and then touch-type paragraphs of text to analyze your speed and accuracy.

Developing Your Touch-Typing Speed

The only ways to develop speed and accuracy are practice and repetition. It's best to focus on your accuracy as you repeat typing drills. Improving your accuracy will increase your confidence, and your speed will develop naturally as a result.

This topic provides you with carefully selected sentences and paragraphs that will help you increase your speed and accuracy. You can use this topic at any time to test yourself and develop your skills. You should also use this course as a reference to go back and work on some of the drills you find most helpful.

Short-Phrase Practice

Use this section to warm up when you begin a practice session. Allow yourself approximately 10 minutes to cover each set of 20 phrases. In this exercise, you will focus on the lowercase a–z keys only. Your goal is to type all the phrases, repeating them as required until you are achieving a steady, consistent rhythm with few errors. Start by focusing on your accuracy. Speed will come with time and practice.

When you practice a long list of drills like the one that follows, always start by checking your posture and finger positioning on the home keys. Make sure you always return your fingers to the home keys between each key you type.

PRACTICING SHORT PHRASES

1. Type the following phrases. Make sure you are looking at your screen, and focus on your accuracy, not speed. Don't worry about capitalization and punctuation in this activity.

   - **when will we start the game**
   - **it could be a long time coming**
   - **come along with me and we will see the game**
   - **the ride was a lot of fun**
   - **she went to work today**
   - **can we come to the school party**
   - **we can see the sun set in the distance**
   - **a bridge is the only way to cross this river**
   - **the river is flowing fast and free**
   - **time waits for no one**
   - **summer holidays are the best time of the year**
   - **you are the last person to see the painting**
   - **they want everybody to enjoy the show**
   - **please discuss your needs with the leader**
   - **once upon a time there were three bears**
   - **living on board a ship is sometimes very scary**
   - **the first time we came over we were very late**
   - **it could be that the engine has stalled**
   - **it tells the story of eight women and one man**
   - **we look forward to welcoming you to our home**

2. Take a quick break to stretch your arms and fingers.

3. Type the following phrases. Make sure you are looking at your screen, and focus on accuracy, not speed. Don't worry about capitalization and punctuation in this activity.

   - **we climbed the mountain path and arrived at the summit at sunset**
   - **the weather in the region was cloudy and raining**
   - **it would be a very long time before we went back**
   - **the zoo was full of interesting animals**
   - **there was peace and quiet whilst the service was in progress**
   - **the quaint cottage sat on the bleak and windswept hillside**
   - **amazingly the race got off to a fast pace**
   - **everyone involved saw the young boy race ahead of the pack**
   - **the horse show was a great success and we all enjoyed the day out**
   - **being in time for class is the best way to stay in his good books**
   - **thanks for your email and for attaching the copy report**
   - **we can send this report to everyone in the sales group**
   - **please let me know when you are going on holiday**
   - **it would help if you could fix the door before you leave tonight**
   - **if we recycle our waste we can help stop global warming**
   - **too many extra lessons make learning very long and boring**
   - **sixteen of us raced past the start line and took up positions**
   - **the cattle were grazing on the long grass and looked very content**
   - **we traveled a long way in the back of the taxi**

4. Take a quick break to stretch your arms and fingers, and check your posture.

5. Continue with the following phrases:
   - **all roads lead to the center of town**
   - **try our ancient remedy for stress**
   - **there is a major new attraction in the theme park**
   - **it is best to be quiet in the library at all times**
   - **a morning tour will include the most impressive buildings in town**
   - **we can make the meeting tomorrow and will bring the report with us**
   - **at last we can see the light at the end of the tunnel**
   - **now the ship had docked we can all disembark and enjoy the beach**
   - **the space shuttle is very impressive**
   - **she was amazed to see no one was injured in the accident**
   - **the last time we cycled to the park it rained cats and dogs**
   - **the clown was funny in his red hat and pointed shoes**
   - **we were told we could eat our supper later if we wanted to**
   - **many people felt the need to go to the church to pay their respects**
   - **service given with pleasure is now the new slogan**
   - **a place to go and stay put for a few days away from the busy office**
   - **all the rooms offer tea and coffee making facilities**
   - **the doctor examined the patient and told her not to worry**
   - **the prices quoted in the brochure are per person per night**
   - **email the different options to her and see what she prefers**

6. Take a quick break to stretch your arms and fingers, and then continue with the following phrases:

    - **the web has truly saved me a great deal of time and money**
    - **business leaders now believe that touch typing helps efficiency**
    - **a visit here is a bit like staying at home**
    - **it was a true story depicted with great understanding**
    - **courage and determination are all you need to succeed**
    - **some people worked a lot harder than others**
    - **we enjoyed the stunning views from the top of the hill**
    - **snow and rain were forecast for the afternoon**
    - **making a list of priorities on a daily basis helps get the work done**
    - **happy customers are what we all strive for**
    - **telephone and mail are being gradually replaced by email**
    - **twenty eight of the boats were built in this shipyard**
    - **being able to touch type without looking at the keyboard is great**
    - **being able to touch type is going to make using my computer more enjoyable**
    - **we all need to be able to touch type so we can focus on our work**
    - **kaz is a very quick way to learn to touch type**
    - **walking in the woodland he could see lots of wild animals living there**
    - **quick and easy is the best way to start the race**
    - **zip along and get me a hot cup of coffee please**
    - **there could be at least twenty ways to complete the puzzle**

7. Take a quick break to stretch your arms and fingers, and then continue with the following phrases:

   - **the exit sign was illuminated with a green and red light**
   - **trains and boats and planes**
   - **a great deal of time is wasted in meetings that are not properly planned**
   - **towns and cities are usually much noisier than the suburbs**
   - **the lazy man was quietly sleeping at his desk**
   - **quick as a flash she jumped over the wall and ran along the street**
   - **maximum effort and concentration are needed to win at this game**
   - **releasing the weight of lead from the boat caused it to sink**
   - **now and then you come across something really new and useful**
   - **the group of children really enjoyed the day at the museum**
   - **shoals of fish came right up to the side of the boat**
   - **we can agree to the terms of this agreement so we can move forward**
   - **meeting up in two weeks time works best for everyone**
   - **playing a musical instrument is a great achievement**
   - **time after time the fox would return for more food at the house door**
   - **she met her best friend after work and went for a meal**
   - **he was really getting the hang of this typing business**
   - **all you need to do is concentrate on typing accurately and speed will follow**
   - **there are many types of software but he liked playing games best**
   - **after this you will feel ready for anything**

8. Take a quick break to stretch your arms and fingers, and then continue with the following phrases:
   - **they celebrated her birthday by inviting friends and family to a party**
   - **bricks and mortar are one of the most popular of investments nowadays**
   - **the building will take just under two years to complete**
   - **they do not seem to have thought of the problems involved**
   - **let us all go and see the animals in the zoo together**
   - **we can all be quiet for as long as it takes to get his attention**
   - **there are easier terms to be found if we shop around**
   - **the proposed network would be modeled on the same one as before**
   - **some people are very cautious before accepting strangers in their home**
   - **the number one expense for most people is taxes**
   - **the ice cream had melted and was running down my hand**
   - **we sat there uncertain of his message**
   - **please expand your point of view so we can all share it**
   - **the two women met with him and left twenty minutes later**
   - **he parked the car and walked up the drive cautiously**
   - **the milk cartons were filled with red paint for the walls**
   - **great opportunities are not always seen with your eyes**
   - **the information pack contains a service guide and a price list**
   - **please read the terms and conditions and get back to me as soon as possible**
   - **let us look at the results of the course**

9. Take a quick break to stretch your arms and fingers, and then continue with the following phrases:

   - **people of all ages from all over the world learn to touch type with kaz**
   - **it is a waste of time and money if he cannot make the meeting**
   - **teachers and students should be able to touch type**
   - **let us spend some time walking around the beautiful gardens**
   - **time and again it was shown that people liked the town shops**
   - **the airport lounge was new and welcoming for new passengers**
   - **takeoff was always an exciting time for the children**
   - **parents had said the school was the best in the district**
   - **why make something complicated when common sense tells you it is simple**
   - **easier times are around the corner**
   - **once it was possible to cycle all the way into town without seeing a car**
   - **will the last person to leave the room please turn out the lights**
   - **so long as we all think it is complicated it will remain so**
   - **now we can visit the zoo any time we want without our teachers**
   - **they all decided to walk up the stairs to get some exercise**
   - **there was a post at every twist and turn of the path**
   - **she would clean her bike every week without fail**
   - **sometimes he was the last person to know what was going on**
   - **please find attached the agreement for your signature**
   - **can you let me know what dates you have free next month please**

10. Take a quick break to stretch your arms and fingers, and then continue with the following phrases:

   - **if you want further information please call my office**
   - **now we know what is needed to plan the campaign**
   - **it seemed as if the people were keen to join in the race**
   - **please let her know where to go to get help and advice**
   - **to apply for a certificate please contact your local office**
   - **it is important that we get this message across**
   - **please make up your mind and let me know what you need soon**
   - **it seemed as if all the children were learning at the same pace**
   - **the steps begin a couple of feet above ground**
   - **she always wants to get her own way**
   - **this is what some people do to their gardens**
   - **any wine lover will find this online magazine a joy**
   - **we are hoping to get a chance to visit again soon**
   - **the weather reports say we can expect hot and sunny weather**
   - **she has many friends in high places**
   - **please be sure to train all the team in the correct procedure**
   - **now that we have the resources we need to set a target for completion**
   - **the man on the train got up to offer his seat to the lady**
   - **twenty three of the fifty people attended the course**
   - **the manager of the division questioned the results**

11. Take a quick break to stretch your arms and fingers, and then continue with the following phrases:
    - **on a hazy day the view is very restricted**
    - **at last the hustle and bustle of the day was behind them**
    - **driving without looking at gears is like typing without looking at the keys**
    - **many of his friends saw his new touch typing skill and were envious**
    - **it could have been the air conditioning that gave him a cold**
    - **she was the best public speaker to come out of the school**
    - **progress is often made by having the time to stop and plan with ideas**
    - **the meeting started with the minutes of the last meeting being read**
    - **he was naturally quite shy and reserved**
    - **he was so happy in his new job**
    - **there is no better feeling than playing at home**
    - **the weekend is what we all look forward to**
    - **she was studying graphic design at college**
    - **the coastal town had replaced all its street furniture**
    - **can you call the customer for their purchase order number please**
    - **it is never too late to learn to touch type**
    - **the world is getting smaller all the time**
    - **we have the network version of kaz for all employees to use**
    - **the intranet version of kaz makes learning really simple**
    - **so far not many of the teachers had received their laptop computers**

12. Take a quick break to stretch your arms and fingers, and then continue with the following phrases:

   - **everyone was looking forward to the next meeting**
   - **if mike jived rude dance**
   - **slap now baggy hat**
   - **it was time to take the extra quiz**
   - **now that we have completed the assignment we can move on**
   - **we need to know how many people will be attending the seminar**
   - **the cat and the dog finally became the best of friends**
   - **sometimes the zoo keeper asked us to keep quiet**
   - **the ship sailed for the next port as the sun was setting**
   - **come along to the next staff meeting if you can**
   - **it was high time the group solved this problem**
   - **all holidays need to be recorded with the manager in advance**
   - **the pilot carefully threaded the aircraft between the low clouds**
   - **they were all amazed at the acceleration of the aircraft**
   - **now was not the best time to be taking a break**
   - **if you have a good idea then believe in it and never give up**
   - **innovation is a necessity not a luxury in business and education today**
   - **affordable accommodation is essential for people working in the city**
   - **trains will need to improve their service if they are to compete**
   - **it is never a good idea to cross a busy main road**

Practicing Complete Punctuated Sentences

Now, you'll start drilling complete sentences. Again, allow approximately 10 minutes to cover each set of 20 sentences. Your goal is to type all of the sentences until you are achieving a steady, consistent rhythm with few errors.

Remember, always start by checking your posture and finger positioning on the home keys. Make sure you always return your fingers to the home keys.

PRACTICING COMPLETE SENTENCES

1. Type the following phrases. Make sure you are looking at the screen, and focus on accuracy, not speed.

   - **The box contained two parcels.**
   - **A class of girls walked to the library.**
   - **Who is she?**
   - **The bird can't fly.**
   - **Peter bought a new CD.**
   - **Jane was sad, but cheered up later.**
   - **Catch the horse.**
   - **Whatever you do, don't feed the penguins.**
   - **Sunshine now, rain later.**
   - **Mike jived all night.**
   - **She wore a baggy hat.**
   - **Wear the dunce hat, she said.**
   - **Extra homework for you.**
   - **The police quizzed the teacher.**
   - **Quickly, come and see.**
   - **It won't matter a bit.**
   - **Be careful, Mr. Smart.**
   - **Introduce me to her tomorrow.**
   - **The relationship had broken down.**

2. Take a quick break to stretch your arms and fingers, and then continue with the following phrases:

   - **Clever Chloe can collect the ball.**
   - **If you always win, then it will be difficult for me.**
   - **Officially, the time had come.**
   - **She took early retirement.**
   - **The bank statement showed a huge overdraft.**
   - **Heavy horses happened to pass by.**
   - **The garden looked lovely in Summer, but bleak in Winter.**
   - **Coal prices went up by 100%.**
   - **The bus carried 28 children, with 2 to each seat.**
   - **Goodness knows what I will do on Saturday.**
   - **He went clothes shopping at the new shopping mall until 2200 hours.**
   - **Well done, Marisa the teacher said.**
   - **He only drinks Chardonnay.**
   - **The men loved playing golf early in the morning.**
   - **The early morning dew glistened in beads on the newly-mown grass.**
   - **Stop! Look! Listen!**
   - **Everyone knows how to play that game.**
   - **Instinctively she turned to go home to her old address.**
   - **Perfect! she exclaimed.**
   - **It hurts to inform you of the truth.**

3. Take a quick break to stretch your arms and fingers, and then continue with the following phrases:

    - **Mr. & Mrs. Johnson frequently went to the zoo.**
    - **The dog was a nuisance, jumping up when visitors arrived.**
    - **The paperboy disliked delivering papers in the early morning.**
    - **Cars, trains, and buses were delayed by the accident.**
    - **How many times do I have to tell you?**
    - **He wanted to change his chintz curtains for velveteen ones.**
    - **Often the clock lost seconds and had to be adjusted.**
    - **All my pencils need sharpening today.**
    - **The fax machine seemed to be continually engaged.**
    - **The shiny paper did not absorb the ink.**
    - **Why don't you go and ask the shop-keeper?**
    - **Too many cooks are in the kitchen.**
    - **Dirty knees need washing.**
    - **I had to clean the carpet regularly in her house.**
    - **The contents' page numbers were wrong.**
    - **The dictionary needed updating every year.**
    - **Good lighting shops are hard to find.**
    - **It belongs to the girls with the plaits.**
    - **Freckles enhanced the little girl's face.**
    - **The little boy blew bubbles on the beach.**

4. Take a quick break to stretch your arms and fingers, and then continue with the following phrases:
   - **The railway station was dirty and in need of renovation.**
   - **Each envelope was steamed open to see the contents.**
   - **The telephone directory did not have the information I required.**
   - **The red car reversed straight into the brick wall.**
   - **The old stone frog looked perfect in the surroundings.**
   - **She only reads biographies.**
   - **Eat your spinach!**
   - **For his birthday, he went to London.**
   - **The woman burned the midnight oil.**
   - **His books were overdue and a fine had to be paid.**
   - **The ambulance arrived to take him to the hospital.**
   - **The cyclist wore cycling shoes, shorts, and a helmet to protect himself.**
   - **Use your vote wisely.**
   - **How do you keep your car so clean?**
   - **Walking downtown became something of a habit.**
   - **It never seemed to rain during the week.**
   - **The smell of cinnamon evoked memories of her holiday in America.**
   - **We have recently acquired a liaison office in our department.**
   - **It didn't seem to matter how many times it took.**
   - **Valentine's Day is on February 14.**

5. Take a quick break to stretch your arms and fingers, and then continue with the following phrases:

   - **They decided to get married at the end of May.**
   - **She could not make an appointment that day.**
   - **Linda had to wait hours in the accident and emergency department.**
   - **The boy fractured his arm when he fell off his horse.**
   - **The cornflowers looked beautiful in the terra-cotta tub.**
   - **The views across the countryside were breathtaking.**
   - **The association met on the second Tuesday of every month.**
   - **Adjust the chair to suit your height.**
   - **Zoology was offered as an alternative at the university.**
   - **Keep knocking those knees together.**
   - **The author could not grasp the ideas.**
   - **The price was $400.**
   - **David gained an impressive 91% in his geography examination.**
   - **The bus driver was often insulted by the passengers.**
   - **It won't matter if you take your sports kit to school.**
   - **Behave sensibly at all times.**
   - **The training course proved too hard for the trainee.**
   - **She eventually turned up with grazed knees and a sprained elbow.**
   - **Anxiously, the mother waited for his return.**
   - **There was a wealth of information available to all who wished to access it.**

6. Take a quick break to stretch your arms and fingers, and then continue with the following phrases:

   - **Go and get six, seven, or eight disks.**
   - **To raise money for charity, Joe said he would walk to raise money.**
   - **It's rare for us to see Mark and Georgina these days.**
   - **I told the maintenance people that the computer screen was pink.**
   - **David was feeling unwell, so he left the office at lunchtime.**
   - **Lyn asked the service engineer to listen to the knocking sound in her car.**
   - **I told them that my name had been omitted from the mailing list.**
   - **My sister hopes to visit Spain in August with her new baby.**
   - **The football team arrived early for the match.**
   - **In order to log on to the system, you must key in your password.**
   - **The first prize in the competition was a camera with a zoom lens.**
   - **The Zurich festival is well known for its jazz bands.**
   - **Max took sixty rolls of fax paper to the exhibition.**
   - **The hotels in Texas are very luxurious.**
   - **The following are on call: Gina, Pam, Claire, and Martin.**
   - **The menu for Monday consisted of the following: soup, quiche, and salad.**
   - **Liz found the journey quite exhausting, but the views were exhilarating.**
   - **All the equipment in the office had to be replaced after the fire.**
   - **The views in the Lake District are disappointing if it is drizzling with rain.**
   - **Mark named his new car 'Blue Bottle Rocket'.**

7. Take a quick break to stretch your arms and fingers, and then continue with the following phrases:
   - **I asked the bank to let me have $200 in Euros.**
   - **Can Jim join us for dinner tonight?**
   - **We are going to an art exhibition while we are in Zurich.**
   - **The company guaranteed next day delivery for an additional $3.00.**
   - **The Museum's display of fine old quill pens was quite extraordinary.**
   - **It would be a good idea to have a color printer installed.**
   - **They were told the job was urgent and that it must be delivered by Monday.**
   - **All the staff were told they must attend the fire drill.**
   - **John rang to say he was sorry but he would not be staying for the party.**
   - **If you want a good career, you must concentrate on your studies.**
   - **We went to the local Health Center to see what information we could get.**
   - **The Casualty Department was busy when we arrived.**
   - **The kitten had knocked all the flowers off the kitchen table.**
   - **Mark, Chris, and Lyn organized a charity fun run in aid of the local hospital.**
   - **The Marketing Manager asked to see all the staff at 1:00 pm.**
   - **The baby was born at 5:20 pm, and they have called her Billy Jo.**
   - **The market sold apples, pears, plums, peaches, and pomegranates.**
   - **The Dr. called in to see the new baby and was very pleased with her progress.**
   - **We are hoping to visit Paris with the children.**
   - **The buzzards were swooping low in the sky and were very impressive.**

8. Take a quick break to stretch your arms and fingers, and then continue with the following phrases:

- **I was amazed to see him driving a bulldozer.**
- **It was a pity to see the dog muzzled, but he had seized the leg of the boy.**
- **The boy's coat had torn, and he looked exhausted when he arrived back.**
- **The hay fever season is upon us and everywhere people are sneezing.**
- **He was abroad on business when his baby son was born.**
- **The bridesmaids were bedecked in blue and yellow ribbons.**
- **The children were fascinated to hear about the journey across the desert.**
- **Don't forget to close down properly before switching the computer off.**
- **People are too lazy to walk and prefer to stay close to their cars.**
- **The views at the top of the mountain were wonderful and worth the effort.**
- **He will need to arrive early to show the new people around the office.**
- **Their flight was delayed, so it was decided to take them straight to the hotel.**
- **The garden area includes a lake and fountain where you can sit and relax.**
- **We caught the next plane back from Venezuela because of the earthquake.**
- **It took 4 people 3 hours to repair the damage to the electricity pylons.**
- **The meeting will start at 3:00 pm, but we hope it will be finished by 6:00 pm.**
- **The marathon is 26 miles long and I was surprised that Sue succeeded.**
- **Elizabeth will be 48 on June 14, and we will have a celebration party.**
- **The bouquet of flowers looked magnificent when it was received.**
- **The Johnsons' vacation lasted three full weeks.**

9. Take a quick break to stretch your arms and fingers, and then continue with the following phrases:

   - **The results were put on the notice board for everyone to see.**
   - **It was not possible to speak to all the students, but 454 were questioned.**
   - **He has decided to take early retirement and I think his wife will join him.**
   - **The new word processing manual was very easy to understand.**
   - **All the manuals are kept in the office cupboard and you must sign for them.**
   - **We climbed to the top of the tower and felt quite dizzy when we looked over.**
   - **The cup of coffee completely covered his keyboard and he did not care.**
   - **The factory works mainly with part-time workers.**
   - **If you want a job, call Mrs. Howell and say I said to contact her.**
   - **Did you call Max to say you would be coming?**
   - **I wanted to fax him but did not have his fax number with me.**
   - **The menu was very comprehensive and quite competitively priced.**
   - **The file was called 'River Hunt' and was not at all exciting.**
   - **The starters were from $3.50 with a main course from $6.50.**
   - **I am always amazed at the equipment on show at the computer exhibition.**
   - **Over a dozen people volunteered to climb the mountain.**
   - **The kids went climbing on their holiday, and they all had fun.**
   - **Francesca won a holiday for two in France; she is planning to go next month.**
   - **There is a special sale on software starting at 9:00 am this Saturday.**
   - **We will need to research the prices to make sure we get a bargain.**

10. Take a quick break to stretch your arms and fingers, and then continue with the following phrases:

    - **The man slipped past security and was not spotted for several hours.**
    - **The apples were a mixture but the cox apple was voted the best.**
    - **There was an alarming accident on the road this morning.**
    - **The traffic was held up for over an hour, but he had his phone with him.**
    - **Can you contact the computer supplies company immediately?**
    - **We need a further one hundred disks delivered before Monday at 9:00 am.**
    - **The Queen arrived at the docks and was cheered by the crowds.**
    - **The hotel has leisure facilities, which can be enjoyed by all the residents.**
    - **We are taking the children to London to see the sights.**
    - **How much did you say you wanted to pay for the china dog?**
    - **Mr. Buxton was in Room 48 but the meeting was in Room 58.**
    - **The sponsored walk was 33 kilometers and 8 of my friends had entered.**
    - **The conference is in Glasgow and will be on text processing.**
    - **We need to know what the shipping costs will be and then fax them.**
    - **We can guarantee delivery within 48 hours but only to a mainland address.**
    - **The contestants were pleased to claim their prize of a holiday in Switzerland.**
    - **Julia Quinnell passed her exams with top marks!**
    - **How quickly can you deliver the goods?**
    - **The holiday for two people was in Canada and was a wonderful win.**
    - **He called the Chairman's secretary to say he was stuck in a traffic jam.**

Speed Drills

Now you will consolidate what you've learned and benefit from the practice you've put in to build your typing speed to 15–20 words per minute.

Practice Typing Paragraphs

Work through the exercises in sequence, and use the practice drills as frequently as possible to increase your typing speed and accuracy. Practicing typing paragraphs is perhaps the best way to hone your touch-typing skills because most of your typing in your profession or hobby will likely consist of paragraphs, rather than short phrases and sentences.

WARM-UP AND ACCURACY PRACTICE

Type each of the following sentences three times. Remember to rest your fingers on the home keys and adopt the correct posture. Concentrate on rhythm and accuracy:

- **It was the first time the Manager has spoken to the group.**
- **Yellow and red were the most suitable colors for the brochure.**
- **They were all very amazed to see the dog jump the fence.**
- **Quick as a flash – the boy ran over the box to the exit!**
- **Why is it that most people when questioned prefer blue?**

Tip: ***Take a quick break to stretch your arms and fingers.***

Measuring Your Typing Speed

If you want to measure and record your typing speed, you will need a stopwatch, a pen, and paper. You can also use the Date/Time clock on your computer to determine your speed. To calculate your one-minute speed:

1. Prepare to start typing, and start your stopwatch or clock. Begin when the timer reaches a point from which you can easily determine when one or two minutes have elapsed.
2. Using the numbers in parentheses at the end of each line of text (below), add up the number of characters and spaces you have typed.
3. From this sum, subtract 1 for each error you make.
4. The average word size is 5 letters, so divide your total by 5 to determine your words-per-minute typing speed.

In the following activity, there is a number at the end of each line of text. This number represents the number of characters in that line of text. The numbers increase with each line.

- It could be argued that workers in zoos are very fortunate to **(61)**
- be able to spend time with animals like foxes, most of which **(121)**
- will never display anything but quiet joy and affection for humans. **(186)**

Assume that you typed the following amount of text, with the following errors (shown in bold):

- It could be argued th**i**t _work**o**rs in zoos are very **g**ortunate to be able to spend t**u**me with anim**l**as like foxes, most of which will never

The line numbers indicate that you typed 121 characters to the end of line 2, plus 10 characters and spaces of the next line, for a total of 131 characters. Subtract 6 for the six errors made, and your total is 125. Divide 125 by 5 (the average number of characters per word), and your typing speed would be 25 words per minute. For a two-minute test, you need to divide your final total by 2 to arrive at your words-per-minute speed. For a three-minute test, divide your total by 3, and so forth.

ONE-MINUTE SPEED CHECK

1. Prepare to start typing.

2. Check your posture, and make sure your fingers are resting on the home keys. If you're timing yourself, open the Date/Time clock and move it to a corner of your screen. Pick a good starting point for the second hand.

3. Begin typing the following paragraph (don't type the numbers at the end of each line). Do not stop typing until one minute has elapsed. If you're practicing this speed drill on your own, begin typing when the second hand reaches the point you have chosen.
   - **It could be argued that workers in zoos are very fortunate to (61)**
   - **be able to spend time with animals like foxes, most of which (121)**
   - **will never display anything but quiet joy and affection for humans. (186)**

4. Calculate your typing speed and record your results.

Two-Minute Speed Check

In the next activity, you will calculate your speed over a two-minute span. Your results might be the same as they were in the one-minute check, but you might find that a test of more than one minute more accurately reveals your words-per-minute typing speed.

1. Prepare to start typing.

2. Check your posture, and make sure your fingers are resting on the home keys. If you're timing yourself, open the Date/Time clock and move it to a corner of your screen. Pick a good starting point for the second hand.

3. Begin typing the following paragraph (don't type the numbers at the end of each line). Do not stop typing until two minutes have elapsed. If you're practicing this speed drill on your own, begin typing when the second hand reaches the point you have chosen.

   - **Council meetings are scheduled for the last day of March, June, (64)**
   - **September and December. The chair person will read the minutes (129)**
   - **from the previous meeting which must be agreed by those present (193)**
   - **before the meeting can begin. Members of the public can attend the (261)**
   - **meetings but space is limited and quickly fills up. The meetings**
   - **have a reputation for lively debates. (364)**

4. Calculate your typing speed and record your results. Remember to jot down that this was a two-minute test.

TWO-MINUTE SPEED CHECK

APPENDIX

Appendix to Part 1

Comments & Suggested Responses

Observing Your Posture

1. No
2. No
3. Yes
4. Yes
5. Yes
6. No

Appendix to Part 2

Comments & Suggested Responses

Check Your Knowledge

1. Press the Spacebar to insert a space between words.
2. Use your right thumb to press the Spacebar.
3. The blinking cursor helps you to quickly see where you are in the document.
4. Press the Enter key to move the cursor to the next line.
5. Use your right pinky finger to press the Enter key.

Additional Reading

Excel 2003 Now! Boston, MA: Thomson Learning, 2005.

PowerPoint 2003 Now! Boston, MA: Thomson Learning, 2005.

Word 2003 Now! Boston, MA: Thomson Learning, 2005.

NOTES

NOTES

NOTES

A P P E N D I X